Eating With The King

A 40-Day Journey to a Godly Attitude Towards Food

Terri Rockwell

*Here I am! I stand at the door and knock. If anyone
hears my voice and opens the door,
I will come in and eat with him and he with me.
-Revelation 3:20*

Xulon PRESS

Dedication

This book is a gift I offer back to the One
who gave it to me as a gift first.
Each time I sat down to my computer, I
knew I had nothing to write.
I pray that every sentence be Your truth to
Your glory.
Anything that isn't You should fall to the
ground and be fatally trampled.
May only Your Word and Your promises be
remembered and praised forever.
I can't wait for the day when I get to share a
feast with You face-to-face, my King.
We will celebrate Radiant Life
together forever.

I also wish to thank my wonderful husband,
who encouraged me to write this for years,
believing God would use my life to help
others.
He was, is, and will continue to be my hero.

May God bless him a hundredfold for all he
has invested in our family.
I love you, Jason.
TP

Introduction

This book is my testimony of God's faithfulness. It's not a diet plan. It's not a quick fix. It's not a do-it-yourself program. It comes from a place of desperation and ignorance.

The Lord Jesus revealed Himself to me in 1999 at the age of 30. It was a miraculous event. I heard His voice say, "Terri, I died for you." No one else could say that. I knew it was Jesus. Scales were ripped from my eyes. My heart cracked into a thousand, no... a million pieces, and the burden of at least that many sins was lifted from my back. I sobbed my way to the front of that randomly-chosen church, confessed my unworthiness of such a Savior, and asked Jesus to be Lord of my life. The burden of the sin I had carried gave way to inexpressible joy. I felt like I was walking three inches off the ground. Suddenly, I could see nature in all its fullness. It may sound cliche, but the sky was bluer; the grass was greener. Everything was alive! I was alive! I knew I was a brand new person.

And I hadn't a clue what to do about it.

Discipleship in God's Word began a year later. I had a lot of joy but not a lot of wisdom. I have overflowing gratitude to God that He sent me a mentor named Julie Paskauskas. In about the time it took me to master spelling her name, we became prayer partners.

It was on the day of one of our weekly prayer times that I learned that my cholesterol was 317. For those of you not familiar with cholesterol numbers, that is REALLY bad. Doctors say that number should be under 200. When I got to our prayer gathering, I was desperate. I thought God and I had a deal. It went like this:

"I don't get drunk. I don't smoke. I don't do drugs. I don't drink coffee. I even exercise! Just let me eat whatever I want."

Clearly from the cholesterol number, the answer was "NO DEAL." You see, God wanted my heart. I had never heard the word "idolatry" in relation to food before. Through Julie and scripture, God revealed that food was an idol in my life. I had meditated on thoughts of brownies, pizza, seafood, and ice cream continuously.

Food was the first thought in my mind upon waking. At breakfast, I was thinking about what I would have for lunch. At lunch, I was planning my afternoon snack, etc. I had restaurant menus memorized. You get the idea. I delighted more in pleasing my tastebuds than in my Savior.

I fell on my face in repentance and set about feasting upon God's Word. Within four months, much to my doctor's shock, my cholesterol was down to 181.

"That just doesn't happen," he said. The same man who four months earlier had told me, "This isn't funny. You could have a heart attack." now proclaimed, "Well, heart disease isn't going to be your cause of death."

Truthfully, I wish I had my cholesterol re-checked the day after I repented because I believe God did the miracle in my blood right then and there. I could feel Him cleaning out my arteries. I could feel my blood flowing freely. I could feel more energy coming to me. I was healed. How astonishing it was to me that the Savior who died for my eternal life was also so intimately concerned with my physical body.

Oh, and I lost 25 pounds in those four months.

But, don't seek Him for that reason! He's worthy of so much better than that! The pure JOY I experienced in the process of learning to be fed by my Heavenly Father far surpassed the thrill of tucking in my shirts and wearing belts for the first time since middle school. (But, that *was* part of the joy that Jesus and I celebrated together.)

Our intimacy at that time was meal-by-meal, moment-by-moment. We celebrated the Lord's Supper all day. It was true Communion as I waited upon Him for true bodily hunger and relied upon Him to show me fullness.

It really was as simple as that. Satan likes to confuse us with many options and complex and costly weight loss plans and programs. Jesus simply says,

*Here I am. I stand at the door and knock. If anyone hears my voice and opens the door, I will come in and **eat** with him and him with me. -Revelation 3:20*

The Bible is called the Sword of the Spirit. I guess you could say this book is a "pocket-knife" of the Spirit. It is a handy scripture reference about food and eating. It shouldn't sit on a shelf but go with you wherever temptation might attack.

Now, I realize that his book is a quick, easy read. You might want to speed read the whole thing at once and just get on with doing it. If you feel led by God to do that as an overview, go ahead. But be careful. Make sure to go back and do the study day-by-day for the full 40 days. You will need that much time and that daily encouragement to stay focused.

They say it takes 30 days to develop a good habit. I think the Bible proves it often takes 40 days to let God complete a good work. Instead of putting the book away when you complete the 40 days, begin again with Day One and keep going. I learned the hard way that breaking a bad cycle means continually renewing the one God wants. When you think you've got it down pat on your own, that's when you will fall. We will **always** have to rely on God.

I hear a knock at the door..... Let's answer it together.

A Note on Exercise

You might want to know right at the starting line what exercise you should do while learning how to rely on God to eat well. Let me share this thought from my personal experience, and then I will give you a scripture to pray through as you decide what God would have you do.

(You see, His beautiful plans for each of us are different.)

When He was taking me through my own process of falling out of love with food, He was very clear that I should NOT engage in heavy exercise. He wanted to show me how to rely totally on Him for a healthy body without being able to take any of the credit myself for the improvements. When people would ask, "Wow, you've lost weight. Are you working out?" I could honestly say, "No. I'm just praying a lot about how I'm eating, and God is showing me how to make my body more healthy." I guess He didn't want my testimony to be jaded. He wanted me to know just how much He cares about my heart towards food without any confusing side issues.

Once He brought my cholesterol down, and I was absolutely convinced that He did it, I was free to work out again. I am an advocate of living an active lifestyle rather than what we think of as "working out." I see people in the gym, looking tortured by the equipment with no joy in their countenances. And, I think, "This is not what God has in mind for His children."

This is the advice the Apostle Paul gave his disciple Timothy:

For physical training is of some value, but godliness has value for all things, holding promise for both this present life and the life to come. -1 Timothy 4:8

I take that to mean physical exercise is good; but spiritual exercise is better.

Just the same as we desire to eat for the glory of God, we should move our bodies for the glory of God with hearts full of gratitude. It doesn't have to feel like it's killing you.

Exercise is worship, too. Do it in a way that pleases Him.

DAY ONE: The Heart Attack

So here we are. You and I are embarking on a journey together, seeking the heart of God and freedom from our common foe. Food isn't the foe. Let's just clear up that confusion right from the start. It's not the brownie's fault.

My heart is the matter. So is yours. They are supposed to belong to God, but they go astray. In our case, they wander to food. That is idolatry. This is a simple truth that will set us free, as we repent and turn our hearts back to the living God, who loves us so much that He sent His one and only Son to die.

> *For God so loved the world, that He gave His one and only Son, that whoever believes in Him shall not perish but have eternal life. For God did not send His Son into the world to condemn the world, but to save the world through Him. -John 3:16-17*

Did you fall for the trap of glossing over that verse because it is so familiar? Go back and read it again after praying for a fresh revelation of the weight of its saving grace for YOU. Fill in your name where it says "the world."

Overcoming overeating is a process of transference. It is fully submitting our hearts to the Holy Spirit and trusting in Him to transfer our love for foods to a love for God. It's as simple as that. All that is required of you is a childlike faith to believe that your Heavenly Father wants your devotion; your Savior Jesus Christ secured your victory on the cross, and the Holy Spirit lives inside you with full power to overcome temptation.

<u>Practical Tip of the Day</u>:
Eat when you're hungry. Stop when you're satisfied.
Don't make it any more complicated than it is.
You are *hungry* when your stomach growls. Don't eat before the growl comes, not even a minute before! (You may have to wait for it on your knees in prayer at first. I did! I promise, it will come!!!!)
Eat slowly, enjoying the company of the King and whomever else He has given you to share the meal. Receive the food thankfully, asking the Spirit to prompt you when your body has had enough.
When you feel that prompting, your body has had enough. Don't question it. Don't take even one more bite. Be satisfied!
This will likely result in you eating a much smaller portion than you're used to. Don't panic!
If you think you didn't eat enough, you can just look forward to your next growl in a few hours.
YOU WILL NOT STARVE BEFORE THEN.

Medical Note: if you need something in your stomach in order to take medicine, have a few crackers or half a banana. Then wait for your next growl.

DAY TWO: Taste and See that the Lord is Good!

A re you already having fears, doubts, and shame about this journey? You're not alone. I am too. We have all felt the shame of trying this diet or that and ending up back where we started. We don't want to drag God into that mess. We've prayed for help before, haven't we?

We let God down, didn't we?

If we're in that mode of thinking, we've put our trust in the wrong place. We've tried to handle it ourselves, maybe asking God for a blessing over *our* effort but not really trusting in *Him* for the deliverance. Today, we allow God's perfect love to cast out all shame and fear.

Rejoice in reading all of Psalm 34, taking special note of what these verses tell us about God's willingness to satisfy our true **hunger:**

I sought the Lord, and He answered me; He delivered me from all my fears. Those who look to Him are radiant; their faces are never covered with shame. This poor man called, and the LORD heard him; He saved him out of all his troubles. The angel of the LORD encamps around those who fear Him, and he delivers them. Taste and see that the LORD is good; blessed is the man who takes refuge in Him. Fear the LORD, you His saints, for those who fear Him lack nothing. The lions

*may grow weak and hungry, but those who
seek the LORD lack no good thing.*
  -Psalm 34:4-10

Practical Tip of the Day:
This will challenge many of us who have
grown up believing that certain foods are
evil:
Eat what you really want.
Jesus declared all foods "clean" in Mark
7:14-19. He's much more concerned about
what comes out of our hearts than what goes
into our mouths. In fact, read Colossians
2:20-23 for yourself. It warns us not to
be tricked by human wisdom that forbids
us to taste certain foods. God knows that
depriving ourselves of certain foods won't
result in a long-term heart change. It only
makes us want them more! Our heart change
is His goal.
When we share His goal, the King delights
in giving us delicious foods from His hand.
He has no desire to deprive His Beloved.
That's YOU!
So yes! Within the prayerful boundaries of
hunger and fullness, enjoy the miraculous
freedom of eating what you want. Make
sure to save room for dessert! Remember,
it won't take much to fill your stomach. Eat
slowly and gratefully, enjoying every bite as
a gift from the
Lover of your Soul.

(You may think that if you eat what you really want, you'll live on brownies and ice cream for the rest of your life. I promise you won't.) God designed your body to want what will make it run the best. Little by little, as you surrender to the Holy Spirit in this area of life, you will desire to eat the foods God wants you to eat. (It won't be tofu and rice cakes either. Again, I remind you that His plan is not for deprivation. It's for delight.)

He made you! He knows you inside and out, better than you know yourself. He knows what fuel is the best for your body. Trust, believe, obey, and rejoice!

The king is enthralled by your beauty; honor Him, for He is your Lord. -Psalm 45:11

DAY THREE: Worshipful Eating

Anything can be worship when we're focused on God. Folding laundry can be worship. Raking leaves can be worship. Eating can be worship. The key is to be focused on the Provider of the food not the food itself.

All too often, we pray a lightning-speed blessing over the food so we can dig in ASAP. Many times we might even be salting the side dish before the blessing is even over! We just can't wait! Oh yes, we can. It's called self-control. It's a fruit of the Holy Spirit. And, if you're a believer in Christ, you have it. We may not have exercised it much to this point in time, but it's available in abundance. We need only to ask the Lord to produce that fruit in our lives and then believe we have received it.

Instead of rushing to eat today, we will make this declaration out loud in faith:

"I don't care about food. It doesn't matter. It's just fuel for my body. It does not rule over me. It does not have my heart. I worship God alone. I will only eat what the Holy Spirit says my body needs to be healthy. God, please satisfy me with your unfailing love today. I love You. I will wait on You to delight me in ways food never has and never will!"

Because Your love is better than life, my lips will glorify You. I will praise You as long as I live, and in Your name I will lift up my hands. My soul will be satisfied as with the richest of foods; with singing lips my mouth will praise You. -Psalm 63:3-5

<u>Practical Tip of the Day:</u>
Until God gives you the growl, use your mouth as an instrument of praise. Memorize some scriptures that speak to your heart. *"My soul will be satisfied as with the richest of foods!"* That was a key scripture for my deliverance. Many times, it accomplished the purpose for which it was sent—to deliver me from temptation to eat before hungry or past full.

I urge you to pray God's Word over your meals. I promise you will find it much easier to resist the urge to "gobble down" your food if you pray this:

God, in view of your mercy, I offer my body as a living sacrifice, holy and pleasing to You. This is my spiritual act of worship. - Romans 12:1

As I told you, this is a process of trans-ference. The Word of God must become what we desire to devour instead of food. Anytime we get rid of something (in this case our gluttony), we have to replace it with something of God, or we will inevitably return to our old ways.

Pray, and dig in! Feast upon God's presence and His Word. Eat the Bread of Life until your heart's content. This is the one thing in life that you can indulge in without limits!

When true bodily hunger comes, invite Jesus to sit and eat with you. Share a sweet time of communion.

DAY FOUR: Desperate Desire

How bad do you want it? Not the food–the freedom from it.

Are you ready to say, "Jesus, You can have it; I don't want it anymore?"

That's when my freedom came; when I no longer fought the desire to overeat. I surrendered it to Him. The first time I actually forgot to eat at a normal meal "time," you could have knocked me over with a feather. That was, for me, the definition of the Promised Land. I wasn't worried about what I was going to eat for a change! Suddenly, in the middle of doing something, my stomach growl caught me by surprise. Hallelujah and yippee! I pray that today, you will realize that freedom is possible, and it IS God's will for you, dear one.

> *Then Jesus said to His disciples: "Therefore I tell you, do not worry about your life, what you will eat; or about your body, what you will wear. Life is more than food....." -Luke 12:22-23*

Jesus couldn't make it any more clear and plain than that, could He? That is a command. Do not worry about what to eat. Life is more than food. Whoa. We don't act like that's true in our super-size-it culture, do we? But that doesn't make it any less true. There's another precious gem of scripture that is very short to memorize but powerful to declare: "*Life is more than food.*"

Practical Tip of the Day

Enjoy sitting down to meals with others regardless of whether you're hungry. Timing out your growls takes a little time, but you'll get the hang of it. You'll start to discern how much of a snack will sustain you until your family is ready for dinner, so that your growl will be in full bloom. God is more than willing to give that discernment. Again, you need only to ask.

Know your company. If you're eating with immediate family members who understand that you're trying to obey God by not eating when you're not bodily hungry, then hold fast. Don't eat just to eat with them. Sit and enjoy their presence. Eat later.

However, if you're at a dinner party where it will be very obvious that you're not partaking of the meal being served, don't be rude! Making a big speech about not being able to eat for the sake of God will not bring Him glory. Just eat a small amount, and try to plan ahead to be hungry for the next occasion. Don't be a stumbling block to others by playing martyr. Yet, don't use your lack of planning as an excuse to over-indulge either. Remember, it's all about your heart before God. He knows the difference between reality and rationalization.

Oh, and you should know, leftovers are OK! Contrary to what our parents taught us, it's not a sin not to clean your plate! Read about

what happened after Jesus fed 5,000 with the
loaves and the fishes.

*They all ate and were satisfied, and the
disciples picked up twelve basketfuls
of broken pieces that were left over. -
Matthew 14:20*

I pray that God will multiply my leftovers to fill the mouths of the hungry
around the world.

He is able to accept my tiny sacrifice
and bless it!

You might even consider boxing up leftovers
for the homeless or to share with a neighbor.

DAY FIVE: Pleasant Places

Today you might be thinking this whole idea is both too easy and too hard. We have been so conditioned to think we need a "diet plan" to eat well. Our minds are blown by the freedom of not counting fat grams, carbs, or calories. We are used to being in control. This approach may feel totally out of control. Good! You're not in control now. God is. You must yield daily to the Holy Spirit's control. You must make a daily declaration to die to the flesh.

> *Then Jesus said to His disciples, "If anyone would come after me, he must deny himself and take up his cross and follow me. For whoever wants to save his life will lose it, but whoever loses his life for me will find it." - Matthew 16:24-25*

New life and new joy are found in denying the desires of our flesh. Yet, even within this simple freedom from God, it is still very hard to wait for true hunger and hard to stop when God says, "That's enough." Be encouraged!

God's ways are simple and orderly. He wants to make this easy on you, but you HAVE to stop trying to do it yourself. Let go. Do it His way. Let Him show you the boundaries.

> *LORD, You have assigned me my portion and my cup; You have made my lot secure. The boundary lines have fallen for me in*

pleasant places; surely I have a delightful inheritance.
-Psalm 16:5-6

Practical Tip of the Day:
Victory may come instantaneously to you. God may choose to deliver you in one moment from the desire to overeat. In my experience though, it was more of a process. Celebrate each victory along the way to freedom. At first, a victory is waiting until your stomach growls just one time! That is HUGE. Celebrate that! You overcame the enemy!!!
The next day, you might have waited for the growl two times. Wow, praise God!
But on the third day, you may have fallen back. It's okay! Don't give up. It's a process. There will be some ebb and flow. Press on!
Throw away your "All-or-Nothing" mentality when it comes to dieting. This is NOT a diet. It's a new way of life. It's not a light switch you turn off when you mess up. Don't let the Devil tell you, "You blew it!" It's not an excuse to wait until Monday, or the first of the next month, or New Year's Day to start again. The Devil loves delayed obedience! That's another way of saying DISOBEDIENCE.
But one thing I do: Forgetting what is behind and straining toward what is ahead, I press on toward the goal to win the prize

for which God has called me heavenward in Christ Jesus.
-Philippians 3:13-14

If you keep going, your victorious moments will begin to outnumber the defeats. Believe it or not, there will come a day that you will be completely victorious. Oh, praise Him!!

Soon, there will be two victorious days back-to-back. Yes, it is coming!

Before you know it, you will have a whole week where you depended on God to feed you.

You will feel better physically and spiritually than you have in your whole life.

When you fall off the horse, get right back up and ride again. You're not riding alone. You're part of the army of heaven! You have got to check out Revelation 19:11-16.

Do it now!

DAY SIX: What Kind of Sorry are We?

Have you ever seen a little boy caught in the act of whacking his sister? Sometimes there is a sincere remorse over hurting someone. He really means it when he says he'll never do it again. Other times, we can witness a whole lot of tears over the upcoming punishment with little intent to change the behavior the next time Sister irritates him.

We're the same way. Sometimes we can weep and wail over our gluttony, but really we just want the bad feeling to go away. We don't want to feel guilty anymore. Can't we just say, "Sorry, God," and get on with life?

Do we really want to give up the love of food? Do we really want to sever that tie to our heartstrings? God knows. He bends down low and listens to what our hearts speak more than what our mouths do. He knows we can fake one but not the other.

Godly sorrow brings repentance that leads to salvation and leaves no regret, but worldly sorrow brings death. -2 Corinthians 7:10

Today we ask God to give us the gift of godly repentance, a true desire to cut the chains that bind our hearts to food. Set us free, O Deliverer! We claim Your promise in Isaiah 61:1 to set the captives free. In exchange, You give us the power to take captives! 2 Corinthians 10:5 says we are to take every ***thought*** captive and make it obedient to Christ. Let's turn the tables on the enemy, shall we? After all, Psalm

23:5 says the LORD prepares a *table* before us in the presence of our enemies! Satan has been bossing us around too long. It's time to take a stand and declare that we are God's children. Young David didn't stand by and allow Goliath to insult the children of God; neither should we!

Practical Tip of the Day:
You want the clearest possible hunger signal. Anything you put in your mouth besides water will have some diminishing effect on that. That includes anything containing sugar like gum, mints, sodas, teas, juices, and coffee.

Water is the best choice between meals if you want to have a good, strong GROWL. I'm not saying you can never drink anything besides water. I am suggesting that you consider sugared beverages as part of your meal, or as a special snack. If a heavy, sugary drink is what you're really craving when the growl comes, have it. But know that when you're done, you're probably going to feel full and have to wait for another growl to eat some real food. If you want to have your coffee after your meal, you're really going to have to eat light in order to save room. (But honestly, I can't condone caffeine. It is addictive. Anything addictive can quickly become something that diverts our dependence on God alone. In plain words, it becomes another idol.)

The bottom line is you have to consider how much room you have in your stomach. It's about the size of your fist. It doesn't take much to fill it, so eat and drink slowly and thoughtfully.

Beverages are not bonuses. They are part of what fills you and must be considered carefully.

When making choices about what goes into the mouth, pray about what will ***truly satisfy***.

Praise God for creating it. Then ***be satisfied.***

DAY SIX (CONTINUED): What Kind of Sorry Are We?

My friend Julie has a powerful testimony about the impact of beverages on weight. I asked her to share it with you here:

I don't ever remember a time that I would have chosen water over a good ole glass of sweet tea-the sweeter the better, or a classic Coca-Cola. I didn't add coffee as my beverage of choice until after my second child was born. I soon learned the only way I could drink it was with just a little bit of coffee, and the rest was cream and sugar. I was drinking one of those three beverages all day long.

After the birth of my third child, I couldn't figure out why I could not get back to my pre-pregnancy weight-which wasn't even my ideal weight. I thought I was following my hunger and fullness cues pretty well. The truth was that I had no idea whether I was hungry or not, because my system was constantly loaded with sugar from the drinks. I knew I needed to cut back especially the coffee, but the thought of it made me sad. After all, it was a social thing...coffee with friends, coffee with my husband, coffee with dessert. Let's be honest; coffee was my dessert.

I heard once, a way to recognize if something was an idol in your life was to ask yourself this question, "Can I give it up?" For me the answer was that I could, but I didn't want to. I had been asking myself this question about six months ago, when I found out some good friends were going through significant marital problems. A friend sent me an e-mail suggesting that I might fast "something" for them to remind me to pray. I knew immediately the "something" was the coffee.

My original plan was to give it up for 40 days. I also decided for the 40 days to give up the tea and coke so I wouldn't just substitute them for the coffee. Of course, for about the first three days, I had an incredible headache, but after that I couldn't believe how much better I felt.

I could actually tell that my stomach was empty and when it was okay to eat. At the end of the 40 days, I had lost 10 pounds. Unbelievable! At that time, I had started an eight week Bible study about eating in moderation. I decided I should hold off on resuming the beverages plus I was scared to go back. I lost another 10 pounds and couldn't believe it because this was the *only* change I made.

At the end of the study, I was still wondering about resuming any of the sugar drinks. Could there be a balance? I still don't know the answer to that one fully. My good friend Terri politely asked if I was crazy. "Why would you go back?" she asked. In my mind, the only way I had given it up was the thought that one day I could drink it again. Over the last two months I've had two cups of coffee at different times, and it really didn't taste that great to me. I weigh now what I weighed when I got married 15 years ago.

God is so good to us! He is such a gentle teacher. I thank Him for the tough times and the hard lessons that only produce that good fruit that will last. The extra bonus is that I prefer water most days and my friends' marriage is in the healing process. As I write this, I'm drinking from a water bottle that Terri gave me in remembrance of what God has done. The outside reads:

> *Whoever drinks the water I give him will never thirst. -John 4:14*

He truly is the only One who will satisfy our every desire!

DAY SEVEN: No Excuses

In the middle of writing this, I went on vacation with my husband Jason and two children, Alexis and Ryan, to Niagara Falls. On the walk from my hotel to the Falls, I passed 3 ice cream shops on one street. All day long, I thought about that ice cream. I'm sure I was begging for it more than my kids, who are 10 and 8. I'm the author of this book; I should know better, right?!

Anyway, instead of being totally and completely focused on God's majesty and power in creating and sustaining those huge waterfalls, my mind kept drifting to how wonderful that soft serve chocolate cone was going to taste on this hot summer day. By the time I got to the ice cream shop, my heart was fixed on it.

My husband ordered a large chocolate-coated waffle cone, so I used that as an excuse to get the same thing. The problem, you see, is that my husband is not lactose intolerant. I am.

I've known it for years. God has taught me very well that a small ice cream cone is delightful; a large causes me terrible stomach pain and ruins my day. I know that, but when I allow myself to meditate on the thought of a particular food, I open the door to Satan to gain control and birth sin in my life.

I fell for the Devil's lies, which manifested as excuses. I'm on vacation. My husband got a large; so should I. I'm truly hungry, so it's okay. The best part is the chocolate-covered cone. I've just gotta eat the ice cream to get to that. I shouldn't waste the money by throwing the rest of this away.

Do you recognize that voice from your own head? We have to know how our enemy works. So here's what God says to fight back when those lying thoughts come:

Live as free men, but do not use your freedom as a cover-up for evil; live as servants of God.
-1 Peter 2:16

Everything is permissible for me—but not everything is beneficial. -1 Corinthians 6:12

Can you see that verse played out in Niagara Falls? Ice cream is permissible, but for the lactose intolerant, it's not so beneficial. Your homework is to read the rest of that passage. (1 Corinthians 6:12-19) It addresses food specifically.

<u>Practical Tip of the Day</u>:
We will find that as our hearts change towards food, it will cause other changes in our lives. We will feel "lighter," more joyful, more peaceful, and even have more money in our wallets! We simply don't need to buy as much food now.
It will change the way we shop. We don't need to fill the refrigerator and cupboards to overflowing anymore because we have no panic in our hearts of starvation. We know

our Heavenly Father will feed us. We also know and accept now that it doesn't take nearly as much food to fill us as we once thought! So we don't feel a need to buy as much.

At a restaurant, we know there's no possible way we can eat a whole dinner portion of anything. We don't even want to! So there again, we save money by either ordering an appetizer as our meal, or by having half an entree to eat the next day for lunch or dinner.

DAY EIGHT: Food is Neutral

Food should be a non-issue in the life of a believer. It's a simple truth. When you think about it, worshiping food is pretty silly, isn't it?

But food does not bring us near to God; we are no worse if we do not eat, and no better if we do.
-1 Corinthians 8:8

Eating doesn't have to be a time of struggle and stress. We have to know and believe with all our hearts that God loves us and wants to take care of us. If we ask, God will give us His eyes to look at the restaurant menu. He will whisper what to order that will truly satisfy. It will be something yummy and something balanced. The right choice will jump out at us.

Yet, we have to ASK.

For everyone who asks receives; he who seeks finds; and to him who knocks, the door will be opened. -Matthew 7:8

This is how our relationship with God deepens. It's through the moment-by-moment communications.....the short conversations seeking guidance about what to eat, and the longer times of heartfelt prayer over a friend's cancer diagnosis. You see what I mean???? It's all about GOD and knowing Him better as we learn to receive His deep, intimate love.

Practical Tip of the Day:
EAT SLOWLY!
TAKE SMALL BITES!
I caught myself chomping off a huge
mouthful of my sandwich at lunch today.
I had to ask myself, "Self...do you think
someone is coming to steal this from you?
What's the hurry????"
Oftentimes, when I am eating in a greedy
way, I will choke. I literally try to swallow
before my food is chewed enough, so I
choke! I know that's God speaking to me.
It's His way of delivering me from the temp-
tation. Here's His promise for you to learn:
God is faithful; He will not let you be
tempted beyond what you can bear. But
when you are tempted, He will also provide
a way out... -1 Corinthians 10:13
Be aware of God's wonderful, precious
WAYS OUT!
They are the escape routes He has prepared.
We are dumb if we don't take them.
It might come as a phone call interrupting a
pig-out moment.
It might be that you actually drop the candy
bar on the floor!
It might be that the steak you order just isn't
cooked to perfection.
Instead of getting angry and demanding a
new steak, you might just thank God for
removing your temptation to eat it all. See
how this is changing us???

DAY NINE: Dancing with the King

I'm a dance teacher, so I have a hard time letting my husband lead when we're dancing together. It looks ridiculous. I struggle against his efforts to lead me because I have a different plan. It's no big mystery why he doesn't dance with me very much. I make us look like we're having a wrestling match instead of a thing of beauty where two bodies are moving as one. All I have to do is give in to his leading.

Now, Mary was a girl who knew how to dance with God. Despite her fears, she moved with the Holy Spirit as He implanted the Savior of the World into her womb.

I am the Lord's servant. May it be to me as You say." -Luke 1:38

What an awesome, obedient, faith-filled, trusting response! Practice saying that aloud.

Doesn't it sound beautiful? It's the will of One becoming the will of two. It's the waltz we are designed to dance with the King commanding the lead around the ballroom.

Now you're thinking: What does all this have to do with eating? It's a picture of how to let God lead your every meal no matter how scary it is to give up control. It must have been pretty scary for Mary, yet she sang a song of praise for the Holy Child within her. Even if it would cost her reputation and her fiancée, she praised God. Within her song are these words:

*He has filled the hungry with good things. -
Luke 1:53*

What did that have to do with being pregnant
by the Holy Spirit? My friend, she was recounting
the faithfulness of her God throughout the ages,
reminding herself that He would not forsake her.
That's the same God you and I serve today. He still
fills the hungry with good things. When He tells you
to stop eating, will you respond as Mary did? "May
it be to me as You say."

<u>Practical Tip of the Day:</u>
SIT DOWN!
It takes about 20 minutes for your stomach
to tell your brain that you've eaten. How
long does your average meal take to eat? 15
minutes? 10 minutes? FIVE??
You can see why it's so critical to eat
slowly. If you eat too fast, your brain
doesn't have time to get the word from
your stomach that it's full. So guess what?
You keep eating....past full.
Also, when we eat too fast, we don't
feel satisfied. Sometimes I can't even
remember eating!
Do not, I say DO NOT, eat standing up.
If Jesus is sharing the meal with you,
would you make Him stand to eat it??? Of
course not!
Do NOT eat out of any food container or
box. You wouldn't hand Jesus a half-gallon

container of ice cream and a spoon and say,
"Have at it."
Fix yourself a plate. Sit down at the table.
Take a deep breath. Give thanks. Eat slowly.
Savor each bite. Eat the best parts first.
Save room for dessert. If you like ice
cream, get yourself a small, cute bowl that
holds one scoop snugly. It will look like
more that way.
Enjoy it! Be satisfied.

DAY TEN: Know Your Temptations

B all parks are not good places for me. I get bored. Eating seems like a good way to pass the time. (Lie) Plus, everywhere around me are the sights and smells of nachos, popcorn, and soft pretzels. It is a Temptation Fest! No actually, it's a Temptation Test.

Will my final answer be, "Everyone else is doing it?" That's not the answer God seeks.

> *Be self-controlled and alert. Your enemy the Devil prowls around like a roaring lion looking for someone to devour. -1 Peter 5:18*

So we can see that "devouring" is not a good thing, let alone a "God thing." When I think of devouring, I picture how my dog eats. It's gross. She doesn't taste a thing. She just inhales it. I don't want to be like that!

If we devour food, totally abandoning self-control, WE will be devoured by the Devil! That's a thought that makes me shudder! I urge you today to write 1 Peter 5:18 on an index card and put it on your fridge, bathroom mirror, or sun visor of your car. Put it somewhere you will see it often enough to memorize it. Have it on the tip of your tongue. It will keep too much food from passing by there on the way to your stomach!

Practical Tip of the Day:

Make a list of your most tempting situations.
I guarantee you there are *times of the day*
when you want to eat for a reason other
than hunger.

I also guarantee there are *places or occasions* when you are tempted to overeat.
I also guarantee that there are stressful
circumstances that cause you to run to
food for comfort.

I can also guess that there are certain
people with whom you feel free (even
expected) to overeat.

I can PROMISE that Satan is well aware
of all these times, places, circumstances,
and people.

He knows what breaks down your self-
control. Do you??????

You have to know to win this war.

For we are not unaware of Satan's schemes.
-2 Corinthians 2:11

Put on the full armor of God so that you can
take your stand against the Devil's schemes.
-Ephesians 6:11

What is this "full armor of God?" We would
be wise to study it in Ephesians 6:10-18.
It is the protection that God offers: security
in salvation, girded in truth, hearts guarded
by faith, made righteous by blood, and
moving forward in peace.
Draw a picture of yourself with the
armor on.

Ask God to dress you in it each morning as
you get dressed.
(Yes, even getting dressed can be worship
when you ask your King what He would like
you to wear.)
YOU'LL LOOK AWESOME!!!!

DAY ELEVEN: Your True Enemy

I t's not the chocolate cake's fault, you know. It can't speak, let alone have the cunning to call me in my sleep. (I'm serious that I used to hear brownies calling to me in my dreams!) The desires of my flesh are strong, but my body isn't even totally to blame for the craving. I know who my true enemy is.

> *For our struggle is not against flesh and blood, but against the rulers, against the authorities, against the powers of this dark world and against the spiritual forces of evil in the heavenly realms. -Ephesians 6:12*

I know some of you aren't comfortable talking about the Devil. It's scary, right? I'm with ya. I'd rather not talk about him either, but the Bible doesn't give me that option. In fact, the Bible commands me to talk *TO* him. When I was a new Christian, that idea freaked me right out the door!

Let me help you as someone helped me at that time. Jesus had, and still has, all authority over all evil spirits. He cast many demons out of people during His ministry on earth. Check out Matthew 17:14-23, Mark 5:1-20, and Mark 9:14-29 for a few examples. Guess what, His followers did too. Read Acts 16:16-18.

You see, right before Jesus ascended into heaven, He passed the torch to us. He gave us all authority to preach, teach, heal, perform miracles, and even cast out demons in His Name. It's all for His glory. So we have no reason to fear Satan or any of his schemes. He was defeated at the cross by the blood of Christ, and we are covered in that blood.

We know that anyone born of God does not continue to sin; the One who was born of God keeps him safe, and the evil one cannot harm him. -1 John 5:18

So how are we to address the Devil when he comes tempting? Two simple things:

1. Tell him out loud that you belong to your Lord Jesus Christ and that he must leave.

James 4:7 says, "Submit yourselves, then, to God. Resist the Devil, and he will flee from you."

2. Do what Jesus did. He gave us the perfect examples in **Matthew 4:1-11.**

With each temptation, you will see that Jesus simply quoted God's truth from the scriptures that refuted Satan's proposition.

Practical Tip of the Day:
Isn't it comforting to know that Jesus was tempted by Satan in the very same way we are? With food! My most practical tip today is to learn to respond to the Tempter the same way Jesus did:

*Man does not live on bread alone, but
on every word that comes from the
mouth of God.
-Matthew 4:4*

Write out these words several times today.
Ask God to tuck them in your heart as your
secret weapon.

Oh, and if you hear a "growl" very soon
after eating, it's just the sounds of digestion,
not a cue to eat again.

DAY TWELVE: The Sin Cycle

S in will lead to death. That's a cold, hard fact we have to accept. My cholesterol used to be 317. That is dangerously high. God showed me that my gluttony was going to result in death if I didn't change my ways to His ways. He came to my rescue. I let Him do the rescuing!

Today, we ask God to break the sin cycles in our lives. The first step is realizing that God isn't causing the problem.

> *When tempted, no one should say, "God is tempting me." For God cannot be tempted by evil nor does He tempt anyone; but each is tempted when, by his own evil desire, he is dragged away and enticed. Then after desire has conceived, it gives birth to sin; and sin, when it is full-grown, gives birth to death. - James 1:13*

Let's read that one over a couple times because frankly, there are a lot of commas and semi-colons to confuse me! Piece this out, and picture the scene in your mind like pregnancy.

Temptation does not come from God. It's our own evil desire that, "drags us away and entices us." Ooh, what vivid images! Once the desire is conceived in our minds, it shows up in our actions, which is the sin. Then if we allow the sin to grow, it will end in death.

God is Spirit. John 4:24 says the Father is looking for worshipers who worship in spirit and in truth. He wants followers who are not spending their time indulging their flesh. We live in a culture where we are taught to get whatever we can to please our flesh...and as much of it as possible before someone else gets it. God says, "No. Let Me provide for you. Trust Me to give you what you're really hungry for: unconditional love, peace, and contentment in your soul."

If we're consistently seeking to indulge our flesh (tastebuds and tummy), we cannot be led by the Holy Spirit. The two are in opposition to one another. They cannot co-exist. They cannot be friends. Nor can we be friends with God and friends of the world at the same time. The world's way leads to death. God's Way leads to life, health, and blessings beyond what we can even ask for or imagine. Choose LIFE!!!!!

<u>Practical Tip of the Day:</u>
I don't care how many times you have messed up so far. Start again. Don't give up! God promises new mercies every day. Sometimes by the time my stomach is growling really hard, I'm so hungry that my mind is a little out of control. Do you know what I mean? It's very important to be in a mode of self-control before you approach your food.
My practical tip is to not wait too long after your growl to eat. Otherwise, you may reach

that fevered pitch that results in eating fast
and overdoing it.

We need a brainwash from the norms of our
culture. We think "full" means we have to
unbutton our pants. No! That's overstuffed.
However, as you progress on this journey,
you will find that sometimes fasting from
food as an offering to God is a marvelous
and unique way to draw closer to Him. Once
again, I remind you that you will not starve
from missing a meal or even fasting for a
day or more.

We'll talk more about fasting when we've
walked a little farther down this road.

DAY THIRTEEN: The Beauty and Benefits of Trials and Temptations

Would you believe me if I told you that it's an honor to be in spiritual struggles? It's true! For one thing, it proves that you are a true believer. To follow Jesus obediently, we have to understand that we will experience the same things He did. We will have to die daily to our selfish desires and be willing to obey the Word of God. It may feel like "suffering" temporarily, but the payoff is earthly health and heavenly rewards that are beyond anything this world has to offer!

> *Now if we are children, then we are heirs—heirs of God and co-heirs with Christ. If indeed we share in His sufferings in order that we may also share in His glory. -Romans 8:18*

It is the very trials and temptations of life that produce the most beautiful changes in our character. They are the very and ONLY things that can truly mold us to be like Christ. Being steeped in self-indulgence will never make us more like Jesus. The tests of forgiving a hateful person, giving to the poor when we don't have much to start with in the checkbook, and being kind to a mentally-ill relative, make us look like Him.

It is a BEAUTIFUL process in the sight of God. To deny ourselves that second brownie because our stomachs are full takes great faith. That is overcoming the enemy! It is faith that pleases God. Right now we ask Him to help us see trials as He does. Father God, help us mature and agree with the refining fire where our faith is made as pure as gold.

Dear friends, do not be surprised at the painful trial you are suffering, as though something strange were happening to you. But rejoice that you participate in the sufferings of Christ, so that you may be overjoyed when His glory is revealed. -1 Peter 1:12-13

Consider it pure joy, my brothers, whenever you face trials of many kinds, because you know that the testing of your faith develops perseverance. Perseverance must finish its work so that you may be mature and complete, not lacking anything. -James 1:12

Practical Tip of the Day:
Take breaks between bites. Put your fork down. Chat a little. Wipe your mouth. Listen intently to someone's story. Have a sip of water. (Don't chug whatever beverage you're drinking, or you'll feel full too soon.) It can be a real battle just to put a fork down. It's a great way to SLOW down your eating. It gives you the upper hand over the Devil. It puts the Holy Spirit firmly in the driver's seat.
Soon, it won't even be hard to do!

DAY FOURTEEN: Don't Worry; Be Happy!

Easier said than done, huh? Worry is eating us alive... literally... with ulcers, and blood pressure problems, and a plain ole lack of joy in daily life. Plus, worry tends to drive us to food because it's at least one thing we feel like we can control in our crazy lives.

Exerting control in any area of our lives will not produce fruit. It's only in the constant surrender of control to God that we can enjoy the peace that passes all understanding. (Philippians 4:7) Once we give the Holy Spirit access to every area, He will produce the self-control we desire over food. You may wonder if it's God's will to do this for you. It is.

His Word says so.

I will not be mastered by anything. Food for the stomach and the stomach for food....
-1 Corinthians 6:12-13

Food is to our bodies what gasoline is to our cars. Simple as that.

Let's ask God today to transfer our worrisome thoughts about what to eat and what to wear to thoughts of worship of Him. I keep telling you this is a work of transference not elimination. We must give God control over our thoughts.

...we take captive every thought to make it obedient to Christ. -2 Corinthians 10:5

What does that look like in my life? When I get a thought like, "I wonder if my husband Jason will take us out to dinner tonight...Where do I want to go? What am I in the mood for?" That is my way of starting to worry about food. I have to stop it right there and put that thought under the rule of Christ. I may say out loud, "NOPE. I'm not going there. I am not worried about what I shall eat or drink because Jesus tells me not to. He will feed me with good things. I trust Him."

He is setting you free little by little. Do you feel it? Hand those thoughts over to Him. Trust Him to complete the good work He has started in you. He loves you with an everlasting love.

<u>Practical Tip of the Day</u>:
When you're enjoying your food, especially things like potato chips or M&M's, don't pop a handful into your mouth at once. It sounds silly to our ears, but try eating one M&M at a time. Bite off pieces of your Doritos rather than sticking a whole one in your mouth. Don't eat them straight out of the bag either. Take a handful, and put them in a bowl. They will last longer if you eat them in bites. Before you know it, you won't even want to finish the whole bowl. You will feel full and satisfied for the treat!
P.S. Don't forget the dip! Yes, if your stomach is growling at 10 p.m., you can have it!!
I enjoyed some just last night.
Where the Spirit of the Lord is, there is freedom. -2 Corinthians 3:17

DAY FIFTEEN: The Pleasure of God

Feeling God's pleasure when you obey Him is the greatest joy there is. No food, no drink, and no drug can compare. I've heard it said, "There is no high like the Most High!"

So if you woke up today fearful of messing up, kick the Devil to the curb and look forward to the joy of obedience instead. Know and believe that your time of testing is coming ever closer to an end. As you more and more consistently obey God about eating, the Devil will give up and move on to another weaker prey. Can I get a, "Hallelujah?"

I've shared 1 Peter 5:8 already on Day 10, but now I want you to gobble up the rest of this slice of the Bread of Life:

> *Resist him (the Devil), standing firm in the faith, because you know that your brothers throughout the world are undergoing the same kind of sufferings. And the God of all grace, who called you to His eternal glory in Christ, after you have suffered a little while, will Himself restore you and make you strong, firm, and steadfast. To Him be the power for ever and ever. Amen. -1 Peter 5:9-11*

Do you see the hope of what's about to happen?? After you have endured this suffering for just a little while, Christ Himself will restore you and make you strong! Oh, and you're not alone. Your brothers and sisters all over the world are being tempted in the very same way you are. Pray for them!!!!! It will strengthen and encourage you while helping them.

<u>Practical Tip of the Day:</u>
Don't allow yourself to praise food with your words. It sounds so weird, doesn't it? That's because it is weird, but people do it all the time.
Let me give you an example from a conversation I heard recently:
"Ooooh...I had this amazing chocolate mousse pie at her party. It was so awesome. It had an Oreo cookie crust as the first layer. Then there was this chocolate mousse. I loved it because it wasn't too sugary or too thick. It was smooth and creamy and SOOO chocolatey! Oh, and the topping. I think it was a cream cheese icing with these beautiful little chocolate shavings on top. It was like heaven!"

See what I'm talking about? Imagine the kind of glory our lives will bring to God when we praise Him in that kind of detail and excitement instead of food! That's exactly the kind of passionate praise He is seeking from us. Thank and praise Him for each layer of blessing in your sweet life with full details of His power, knowledge, and unmatched love, revealed in every situation and circumstance.

You'll never have enough words to adequately describe Him, but He loves it when we try!
Here's a personal motto for you:
Love God. Love people. Like foods.

DAY SIXTEEN: Heart Motive

Why do you want to lose weight anyway?
It's a question worth asking yourself. It may have everything to do with why we're overcoming in this area or not.

If it's for vanity reasons, like how good you're going to look in that dress or how jealous everyone at the class reunion will be, God is probably not very interested in that.

Charm is deceptive and beauty is fleeting, but a woman who fears the LORD is to be praised.
-Proverbs 31:30

On the other hand....if you want to lose weight to give glory to God through your testimony of His power in your life, you're in line with His will and purpose. If you want to be healthier and stronger so you can serve Him, you've got His ear when you pray for help.

Adopting this attitude in a genuine way is a process. It goes against our human nature. (I still find myself backsliding into old, yucky motives about how I look in my clothes sometimes.) We must pray for God to give us His heart–to plant a sincere desire for His glory and attention, not our own. This is one of my all-time favorite verses:

*So whether you eat or drink or whatever you
do, do it all for the glory of God.
-1 Corinthians 10:31*

That's another one of those one-liners that you've
just got to commit to memory. It has the power to
rescue you from so many kinds of bad choices
including overeating. You know by now, don't you,
that God's Word has powers that we can't explain?

*The word of God is living and active. Sharper
than any double-edged sword, it penetrates
even to dividing soul and spirit, joints and
marrow; it judges the thoughts and attitudes
of the heart. Nothing in all creation is hidden
from God's sight. Everything is uncovered
and laid bare before the eyes of Him to whom
we must give account. -Hebrews 4:12-13*

Yes, He is fully aware of our motives for wanting
to lose weight. God's Word is the way to a right spirit
within us.

<u>Practical Tip of the Day</u>:
Eat the best bites first.
Let go of the, "Gotta clean my plate"
mentality.
Survey your plate and decide what is your
very favorite. Eat that first.
And you know something? If you really
want a special dessert, but you're afraid you
won't have room, eat IT first! There are no

rules to bind you except to make sure your
body is truly hungry, and that you don't eat
beyond God's cue of fullness.
Embrace that freedom once more right now,
and thank God for making it **easy** for you!

DAY SEVENTEEN: Glorious Bodies

N ow that we have the heart motive issue straight-
ened out, I have more Good News for you! You
will soon have a glorious body! God's Word promises it. I'll prove it in a minute.

But first I must declare...this life is very short.
When she teaches Sunday school to elementary children, my friend Sophia describes this life as our pinky
fingernail and eternity as the rest of our whole body.
I like that illustration. It keeps my mind on heavenly
things, which lines me up with God as you're about
to see.

> *...many live as enemies of the cross of Christ.*
> *Their destiny is destruction, their god is their*
> *stomach, and their glory is in their shame.*
> *Their mind is on earthly things. But our citi-*
> *zenship is in heaven. And we eagerly await*
> *a Savior from there, the Lord Jesus Christ,*
> *who, by the power that enables Him to bring*
> *everything under His control, will transform*
> *our lowly bodies, so that they will be like His*
> *glorious body. -Philippians 3:18-21*

O God, may our god never again be our stomachs! We are friends with the cross of Christ. We
praise You for it! We do eagerly await our Savior
from heaven, Jesus Christ, who will once and for all
satisfy our desires for glorious bodies that will never
wear out, grow old, get tired, or die! (Does anyone
else just want to jump up and down over that?)

Practical Tip of the Day:
If you're struggling to wait for your stomach to growl, here is a checklist of things to help in priority order:
1. Get on your knees and call for Jesus to come help you.
2. Read a Psalm out loud.
3. Sing a song of praise.
4. Call someone who will pray with you.
5. Call someone who needs to hear your voice.
By then, the temptation will probably have passed, but if not, chew a piece of sugarless gum.
Temptations come, and temptations go. They don't go on indefinitely. When you stand firm, they will go.
(That doesn't mean that Satan won't ever come back and try to stir up your old ungodly desires for overeating. He will, but we'll talk about that more later.)

DAY EIGHTEEN: List the Lies

If you're reading this book, you have come seeking freedom from lies. We've all believed some kind of lies at different times. The enemy came selling poisoned apples, and we bit off more than we could chew. Like Snow White, it's left us in a sleep state spiritually-speaking. We have been rendered helpless but can't figure out why.

Well, here's your wake up call! This is the day you go free. This is the day you allow God to reveal the places where you have bought into lies and have lived your life according to them. This is the day the Prince of Peace comes to wake you with a kiss!

If we've attached ourselves to any ideas or put our trust in anything besides God, we've sinned and need to repent.

Do you believe some human has a better diet plan for your body than God who made your body?

Do you believe yummy foods that contain sugar or fat are inherently evil?

Do you believe it's healthy to stuff your stomach past its limit even if it's with broccoli?

Do you believe it doesn't matter to God how much you eat because "you aren't hurting anyone?"

Do you believe it's alright with God if you eat as much as you want because you exercise?

Do you believe the only way to know if you're being "good" is to count a number on a food label or on the scale?

Do you believe you "deserve to eat" when you've had a hard day or accomplished something?

We've all bought into these or variations of them. I'm a living, breathing testimony that they are all lies. Please stop now and make yourself a list of your best excuses for overeating.

Ask God to reveal any others that only He knows.

Then burn it! Consider it a "burnt offering!"

Let's replace those with some truths. Go read the scriptures for yourself.

TRUTH #1: We have been rebellious, but at this moment, we no longer reject the Lord's instruction. (Isaiah 30:9-14)

TRUTH #2: God's plan is perfect because He knows every inch of our bodies and how they work best. (Psalm 139:13-16)

TRUTH #3: God doesn't place a heavy burden on us. He doesn't require us to tally up points on a food plan or to study food labels in fear.

Come to me, all you who are weary and burdened, and I will give you rest. Take my yoke upon you and learn from me, for I am gentle and humble in heart, and you will find rest for your souls. For my yoke is easy and my burden is light. -Matthew 11:28-30

Practical Tip of the Day:
Share!
We tell our children that all the time, but
when it comes to our treats, we grown-
ups can get downright greedy. Like
the seagulls in Finding Nemo, we say,
"Mine! Mine! Mine!"
Part of letting go of this stronghold means
letting go of the right to say, "Mine!"
You will feel freedom flood over you when
you say, "You want to split this with me?"

DAY NINETEEN: Sin Hangover

Y ou've heard the saying, "Confession is good for the soul." It really is. It doesn't have to be to a certain priest in a certain room, but we followers of Christ have to make a practice to owning up to our mistakes before God and others.

He who conceals his sins does not prosper, but whoever confesses and renounces his sins finds mercy. -Proverbs 28:13

Make a daily, even moment-by-moment, practice of confessing sins to God. You will experience His love and compassion in greater measure. Ask Him daily to reveal any sins you committed unknowingly. It's hard, yes, but so wonderful at the same time because God always forgives. Let me say that again. **God always forgives**. We don't have to walk around with a sin hangover.

If we claim to be without sin, we deceive ourselves and the truth is not in us. If we confess our sins, He is faithful and just and will forgive our sins and purify us from all unrighteousness.
-1 John 1:9

And, there is some undeniable connection between unforgiven sin and health problems. Not in every case, but it's something we are wise to ponder when we are sick or hurting.

Therefore confess your sins to each other and pray for each other so that you may be healed.
-James 5:16

Did you notice the "so that..." part? It ties together confession and healing. King David gives us an example of how bad sin can make us feel physically. Read Psalm 38.

I don't believe **every single sin** needs to be confessed in the presence of another person. If I think of kicking my dog, I can confess that ugly thought to God alone. However, God's Spirit will direct me to confess to another in several situations:

1. If I've hurt someone. I need to ask their forgiveness and make it up to them in any way possible. That's called "restitution."
2. If I have a stronghold starting in my life, He will direct me to pray with an accountability partner to whom I give permission to ask about my temptation in the future.
3. If my sin struggle can help someone else confess their sin. This one is revealed by the Holy Spirit. He may just prompt you strongly to confess your sin to another person because He knows they are struggling in the same way. Your open confession will help them to bring their sin into the Light so they may be healed.

<u>Practical Tip of the Day</u>:
The scale is not your friend.
Don't listen to it to judge your worth or your success in this area.
Don't weigh yourself more than once a week unless God clearly tells you to for His purpose.
You will know if you are being obedient or not without the scale.

DAY TWENTY: Halfway Home

I can't believe we're halfway through our journey already! So, how are you feeling?

I pray right now that you are aglow with the power of the Holy Spirit. I pray that your very countenance has changed because you have been spending so much time in the presence of God. People are starting to ask questions about why you seem different.

The joy of the LORD is your strength. - Nehemiah 8:10

Perhaps to you, my words are foolishness. You don't think they apply based on the way you've been eating. Well, consider that I am speaking in faith to things yet unseen.

I'm not putting my faith in your ability, you see?

I'm putting my faith in God's ability. If you do the same, you will be victorious. Hand it over. Tell Him you don't want it anymore. In fact, you don't want any MORE when it comes to food. You just want MORE Jesus!

I know it's not as easy as I make it sound to find that secret place where Jesus meets with you. Believe me, I know. I have walked through long periods of drought and wilderness in my journey too. There are so many distractions and worries and activity that keep us from being able to take the time to find the secret place. But that doesn't mean it doesn't exist, or that it isn't possible, or that Jesus isn't willing and waiting. **He is.** The truth is that most of the time we aren't willing to give up the other things that are in the way. We don't seek with all our hearts. We give a half-hearted attempt at prayer, worship, or Bible study. He wants our ALL.

You will seek me and find me when you seek me with all your heart. -Jeremiah 29:13

I love those who love me, and those who seek me find me. -Proverbs 8:17

.....he rewards those who earnestly seek Him. -Hebrews 11:6

God's mercy is always fresh. I am claiming victory for you. Though I don't know you by name, God does. He hears my prayer for you today into the future when you are reading this. Isn't that cool? He is not bound by a Timex.

Practical Tip of the Day:
Shackles will fall off you.
I hope and pray you have experienced this by now, so I can confirm it. If you haven't, know that God will do this for you, too. Sometimes when His Word causes a revelation through the Spirit, you will literally feel pounds fall off you in a moment. ***That's*** the time to check the scale to document the work of God for your testimony to share with others.

As you obey God's Word and His commands, He will bless. I had days where I would take a truth deep into my soul and would lose five pounds in a single day. That's the shackles falling to the floor! Be expecting this miracle.

DAY TWENTY-ONE: Spoon-Feeding or Feasting?

S o which is it? Are you letting me spoon-feed you God's Word, or are you feasting upon it yourself? GO READ YOUR BIBLE!

You know I can't do this for you. This is between you and God. I'm just called to come alongside you and encourage you with my gift of faith. I don't have all the answers. The Bible does. My prayer is to offer you enough scripture in this book to increase your appetite for the Book of Life!

Like newborn babies, crave pure spiritual milk, so that by it you may grow up in your salvation, now that you have tasted that the Lord is good. -1 Peter 2:3

Maybe this isn't your first time reading this book. Congratulations! I am so proud of you! It's designed to be read over and over as a tool for continued victory in Christ. But if you're re-reading it because you're struggling, take heart! God knew this would be happening. No matter how many times we fall, He honors our faith to keep trying to please Him. His Word says a righteous man gets up after falling for the seventh time! That means even while we are falling and rolling around in the mud, God still calls us righteous because of the blood covering of His Son.

We just have to keep getting up!!

Getting up demonstrates great faith. That is what pleases God.

Without faith it is impossible to please God, because anyone who comes to Him must believe that He exists..... -Hebrews 11:6

Practical Tip of the Day:
Slowwwwwwww
dowwwwwwwwnnnnnnnnn....
I got a speeding ticket, and I am so thankful for it!
It slowed me down in more ways than one. In slowing down the speed of my car, I also experience a slowing of the frantic pace of the thoughts in my brain. Not in a lethargic, dim-witted way, but in a "God's peace" way.
Do not be anxious about anything, but in everything, by prayer and petition, with thanksgiving, present your requests to God. And the peace of God, which transcends all understanding, will guard your heart and mind in Christ Jesus. -Philippians 4:6-7
This translates to eating. I sometimes race to the kitchen the second my stomach growls, but I find greater power from the Spirit to take it slow. This is what victory tastes like.
Where are you still having trouble? Is anything distracting or confusing you? It may have nothing to do with your weight or food. It may seem totally unrelated, but it's not.
Ask God to reveal it, and deal with it.

DAY TWENTY-TWO: Wonderfully Made

No two of us are alike. In the whole history of the world, there has never been another you. There never will be. That's astonishing to me. What creativity! What intelligent design!

God is totally awesome.

Because of that, no two of us are going to go through this freedom process in the same way. I feel like some may be asking, "When should I be getting the hang of this?" It's normal to want to compare, but not fruitful. We are wise to keep a proper perspective. God is all-powerful. We have no power apart from Him. We are humble. He is exalted. He is completing a good work in us in His timing, which may be different from others.

I will share this about my own journey. I did not think my stomach had the ability to growl. I had never let myself get that hungry before!! It took me quite awhile to let myself get all the way to a growl. I can't remember exactly, but it was probably two weeks. I hit my knees many times trying to wait for it. I think I had tears in my eyes the first time I actually heard the growl!

That was the first step in the process for me. Finding full was a completely different story. Hungry has a definite beginning, feeling, and sound. Full is much harder to find for me.

Your experience may be different. In my journey, I think several more weeks went by before I actually felt like I stopped eating when God said to. It seemed like so much LESS food that I was used to eating. It was!!! But boy, did I feel great! God began to strip the years off of me.

I was in my mid-30's at the time. I literally felt better than I did in my college years and 20's.

He even showed me a new way to wear my hair. It was such a precious time! I felt like Cinderella, getting the makeover by the Fairy Godmother, only this was better. It was a makeover from the inside-out by the very hand of God. I even found a T-shirt in the Christian bookstore that said those very words! I know He put that there for me too. He will show up in every detail of our lives when we are seeking Him with all our hearts.

Seek first the kingdom of God and His righteousness, and all the rest will be given to you as well. -Matthew 6:33

Delight yourself in the LORD and He will give you the desires of your heart. -Psalm 37:4

<u>Practical Tip of the Day</u>:
Chew in the front as long as possible!
Yep, as weird as that sounds, keeping the food towards the front of our mouths will help us enjoy the flavor longer as we take our time to savor each bite.
Remember, we aren't taking as *many* bites any more. So, we have to make them last in order to feel satisfied when the meal is over.

Fight the tendency to swallow immediately.
Your digestive tract will thank you for
making its job easier by chewing the food
more thoroughly. It's all things working
together for good!
*And we know that in all things God works
for the good of those who love Him, who
have been called according to His purpose.
-Romans 8:28*

DAY TWENTY-THREE: Heaven's Honey

One evening, I watched my friend Julie push away a piece of cheesecake that she wanted. I had been slipping in my personal obedience, and God used that to show me again what victory looked like. It's that moment where in God's power, you say, "NO" to the temptation to eat beyond full. You feel so close to God in that moment!

Give us aid against the enemy, for the help of man is worthless. With God we will gain the victory, and He will trample down our enemies. -Psalm 60:11-12

It was such a sweet moment to witness God's pleasure upon Julie. She didn't need any man's help. Her faith in His care outweighed her fleshly desire. It was sweeter than honey. God's Word has a lot to say about sweet honey. It's no wonder the Promised Land was called the land of milk and honey!

Pleasant words are like a honeycomb, sweet to the soul and healing to the bones. -Proverbs 16:34

I have not departed from your laws, for you yourself have taught me. How sweet are your words to my taste, sweeter than honey to my mouth! -Psalm 119:102-103

We are to delight in the sweetness of God's commands. They aren't there to take all our fun away! They are there to protect us, bless us, and guide us to receive God's very best (which is better than anything we can imagine). We can take God at His Word. He never breaks a promise, and His Truths will never prove false or unreliable. How many people can you trust like that? No one. That is why King David delighted so much in God's Words.

If we delight in the sweet treats instead, there is surely trouble to come.

If you find honey, eat just enough—too much of it, and you will vomit. -Proverbs 25:16

We can see that God doesn't forbid the sweet treat. He just warns us about the quantity!

<u>Practical Tip of the Day:</u>
Butter, blue cheese dressing, bacon, hot fudge, sugar....These are ***not*** forbidden foods.
The key is the quantity. God has given them for us to enjoy in moderation with self-control.
Since you died with Christ to the basic principles of this world, why do you submit to its rules: "Do not handle! Do not taste! Do not touch!" These are all destined to perish with use because they are based on human commands and teachings. -Colossians 2:21-22

We, in Christ, do not conform to rules made up by men. We live in the freedom of the Spirit.

So, enjoy a loaded baked potato, a taco salad with plenty of sour cream, or a supreme pizza!

Just make sure you're truly hungry, and stop when God says so.

DAY TWENTY-FOUR: Different Food

We're making a shift in the spiritual realm. That shift is causing ripples on the earth. Can you feel it? Our obedience to God will always impact others. That's the divine plan. Sometimes it will inspire someone to repent and obey as well. Other times our obedience confronts people in a way they're not ready to deal with yet.

They may respond with ugliness. It could come out as veiled insults about our "too thin" appearance, or a "you think you're better than everyone now" jab. It could come under the guise of concern with a question like, "When are you going to stop?" The answer of "Never" may actually cause them to suspect anorexia. It's tough.

I suspect every person who purposes in their heart to eat as God instructs (like Daniel did in Daniel 1:8) will face someone who tries to force food upon him. Daniel wasn't trying to get in anyone else's business. He wasn't trying to push his convictions on anyone else. He just didn't want to eat the king's food and wine, which were against the commands he'd received from God.

(We would be wise to take a page from the Book of Daniel in this regard. We can't force anyone to eat as we do now. We can't preach at them and ask, "Are you really hungry? Aren't you full by now?" It has to come out of a genuine heart change for them. You will know when someone is asking questions out of that sincere desire to know a better way. Then you can share what God is doing in your heart, soul, and body.)

Now, back to Daniel, who was a captive in Babylon after King Nebuchadnezzar conquered Judah. The king assigned Daniel to eat a daily amount of food and wine from the king's own table. You have to figure this was the most yummy food and wine in the kingdom of Babylon. He was forcing it upon him because the king figured he knew best about what would make Daniel a strong servant. He was wrong. You've got to go read Daniel 1:1-21 for yourself to see how God worked in the situation by using **food**.

Would you believe that people even tried to force food upon Jesus?! John 4:31 speaks of an occasion where His disciples were "urging Him to eat." Jesus responded this way:

I have food you know nothing about. My food is to do the will of Him who sent me and finish His work. -John 4:32, 34

It comes down to a question of who's opinion do we value most? God's? Or a person's?

We are fed; we are nourished and full when we do God's will. Eating becomes a secondary activity rather than a focus of daily life.

Practical Tip of the Day:
Rock around the clock!
So many people have told us the lie that you can't eat during certain times of the day.

I'm here to tell you the truth: If your
stomach is growling, your body can
handle food.
If it's midnight and you start growling, eat
what your body calls for.
Stop when God says, "Enough."
You don't have to *sneak* it, like so many
night-feeders do in the shame and cover
of darkness.
If you're hungry, eat. There is no shame.
There is no secrecy before the eyes of God.
You are FREE!

DAY TWENTY-FIVE: Smiley Face Stickers from our Father

This is kind of silly, but I pray it will help you progress on this journey. Each time you either wait to eat until true hunger arrives, or you stop eating when God says, "Enough," picture Him putting a smiley face sticker on your forehead! You get to wear around the pleasure of God all day! By the end of the day, maybe you will have five or six of them. Wow!

It's a good way to check with God after your meal and ask, "God, did I obey You?"

If not, repent immediately. If so, receive the smiley face! He has an unlimited supply and freely gives to all who obey. We are in charge of what we put in our mouths. We no longer dance to the Devil's tune. Our master is Christ. Sin has no power except that which we give it.

Direct my footsteps according to your word; let no sin rule over me. -Psalm 119:133

(Another awesome memory verse to have at the ready!)

Therefore do not let sin reign in your mortal body so that you obey its evil desires. Do not offer the parts of your body to sin, as instruments of wickedness, but rather offer yourselves to God, as those who have been brought from death to life; and offer the parts of your body to Him as instruments of righteousness.

For sin shall not be your master, because you are not under law, but under grace. -Romans 6:12-14

Today, I encourage you to give your body back to God. It has always belonged to Him anyway. But, today, you come fully into agreement with your body being the place where God lives.

Do you not know that your body is a temple of the Holy Spirit, who is in you, whom you have received from God? You are not your own; you were bought at a price. Therefore, honor God with your body. -1 Corinthians 6:19-20

That price was the blood of Jesus Christ. We have to really let that sink in today. Jesus paid for us with His life. He made it possible for His Spirit to abide INSIDE of us. That's an amazing, awesome, astonishing fact! What He asks in return is that we treat our bodies well because they are His holy dwelling place.

Practical Tip of the Day:
There is no rule about how many times
a day you should eat.
Again, each of us is different.
Personally, I eat about four to five
times a day:
Breakfast, mid-morning snack, lunch, mid-
afternoon snack, and dinner.

Sometimes I skip the morning snack if I'm looking forward to a special lunch.
I'll skip the afternoon snack if I know I'm making an early dinner. If my husband is going to be home late, we have a snack knowing we'll have time to wait on another growl for dinner.
Depending on what I eat for dinner and how late I stay up, I may have a snack before bed.
I don't like to try to sleep with my stomach growling. If I'm too tired to get up for a bowl of cereal, I know that God will just take that extra fat reserve off my thighs while I sleep!
Glory!

DAY TWENTY-SIX: No Wiggle Room!

Have you heard the saying, "If you give him an inch, he'll take a mile?" That's Satan all right. His lying whispers will try to steal our hearts from God a millimeter at a time. See, he's far too crafty to just suggest we give up altogether in one catastrophic crash. No, no, He gently whispers suggestions about ever-so-slightly moving the boundary line God has set.

It's been his same game since the beginning of time. "Did God *really* say......?" And guess what the first temptation on the face of the earth was......food.

Now the serpent was more crafty than any of the wild animals the LORD God had made. He said to the woman, "Did God really say, 'You must not eat from any tree in the garden'?"
-Genesis 3:1

Let me give you a personal example of how he tries to move my obedience boundary lines. I know God wants me to get up and spend time with Him at 6 a.m. each day. He's made that very clear on many occasions. Periodically, Satan comes along at 6 a.m. and says, "Did God *really* say to get up at 6 a.m.?" Surely He wants you to get enough rest. Surely He doesn't mind if you sleep until 6:15 a.m." Then guess what, a few days later after I'm in the habit of getting up at 6:15 a.m., he comes along and suggests that 6:30 a.m. really isn't any different than 6:15 a.m. He keeps suggesting a subtle shift that doesn't look or feel like outright disobedience to God.

It has gone on like that at times in my life until one day I realize I'm in the habit of getting up when my children come and WAKE me up at 7:30 a.m. or 8 a.m.! And at that point, it's nearly impossible to have true solitude with Jesus. The house is simply bustling with too much activity. Satan's mission was accomplished.

We cannot give Satan any wiggle room. I can promise you, if he thinks you'll wiggle, he'll do his best to wiggle ya.

> *Therefore my dear brothers, stand firm. Let nothing move you. Always give yourselves fully to the work of the Lord, because you know that your labor in the Lord is not in vain.*
> *-1 Corinthians 15:58*

When you prove by your steadfast obedience that you mean business, Satan will move on. He only has a finite number of demons to dispatch, and he knows his time on the earth is short. He won't waste time on you if you refuse to be moved.

<u>Practical Tip of the Day:</u>
Run!

When the temptation is upon you, get away! If it's mid-afternoon and you're at home just dying to break into a bag of Oreos while the

kids are napping, go sit outside and praise
God for His creation!
If you're at work and the office gang is making
plans to eat lunch at a place where you know you
tend to overeat, ask God who you might invite to
lunch at a different restaurant.
If it's after supper and you're craving a second piece
of blueberry pie, run for the door!
Take a walk. Go visit a lonely neighbor.
Do whatever is necessary to get out of the
situation.

DAY TWENTY-SEVEN: Never Bored

There is no excuse to get bored while we're in this world. There are too many critical prayer needs. There's no time to lose either.

Be joyful always; pray continually; give thanks in all circumstances, for this is God's will for you in Christ Jesus. -1 Thessalonians 5:17-18

Do you ever question whether you are in God's will? Well, there you go! You can be certain you are smack dab in the center of His will if you are joyful, praying, and thankful.

I'm telling you, His ways are clear and simple. WE make them complicated and hard.

So prayer is the perfect anecdote to boredom eating. The Proverbs 31 Woman keeps too busy to mindlessly nibble in the kitchen.

She does not eat the bread of idleness. - Proverbs 31:27

To me, that says this gal doesn't get bored. (How could she with all the sewing, cooking, serving the poor, and buying of real estate?) We will do much better in our eating behaviors if we too stay busy. Not too busy to pray– too busy NOT to pray! This doesn't mean you have to run all over town like a crazy person. It just means that "doing nothing" isn't the blessing so many of us think it is. We want to just kick back and "do nothing." Now, if that's taking time to rest and refuel in God's presence, that's great. More often than not, we just want to veg out.

That's what gets us in trouble with food sometimes. Busy hands don't have time to dig into a bag of chips.

Make it your ambition to lead a quiet life, to mind your own business, and to work with your hands, just as we have told you, so that your daily life may win the respect of outsiders and so that you will not be dependent on anybody. -1 Thessalonians 4:11-12

Practical Tip of the Day:
Use extreme caution near any screens.
Not window screens.
No....TV screens, computer screens, video game screens, or movie screens.
They tend to zone us out mentally. When we're zoned out mentally, we eat mindlessly.
TV watching seems to go hand-in-hand with mindless munching.
At the movies, how can we possibly make it through the two hours without eating a whole tub of popcorn and a sweet snack to balance it out?
We can!!!
We just have to be mentally prepared and aware of the temptation in order to reject it.
We can watch TV or movies without a snack if we're not hungry.

If we can't, then we should find something
more productive to do.
(Did I mention the need for prayer????)

DAY TWENTY-EIGHT: Bread of Life

This is a hard teaching. I know because the scriptures actually call it that. In John, Jesus describes Himself as the living bread that came down from heaven.

Then Jesus declared, "I am the bread of life. He who comes to me will never go hungry, and he who believes in me will never be thirsty." -John 6:35

So far, not so hard. We can accept that Jesus provides what we need to stay alive. But it gets tougher. In fact, upon hearing this, many of His disciples deserted Jesus because they couldn't accept it. Here goes.

Jesus said to them, "I tell you the truth, unless you eat the flesh of the Son of Man and drink His blood, you have no life in you. Whoever eats my flesh and drinks my blood has eternal life, and I will raise him up at the last day. For my flesh is real food and my blood is real drink. Whoever eats my flesh and drinks my blood remains in me, and I in him. Just as the living Father sent me, so the one who feeds on me will live because of me." -John 6:53-57

I'm not even going to attempt to interpret that for you. I just know God wanted me to include that passage in this page. If you are struggling about symbolism versus a literal translation of eating and drinking flesh and blood, go to God and talk to Him. It's an important issue to settle in one's heart because as I mentioned, many disciples no longer followed Jesus after this teaching. Will you?

"You do not want to leave too, do you?" Jesus asked the Twelve. -John 6:67

Simon Peter said he didn't have any place else he could go for words of eternal life. Neither do I. I'm sticking with Jesus. How about you?

<u>Practical Tip of the Day:</u>
Hunger and even fullness are black and white states of being.
We have been made to think they are grey areas, but that's a lie.
If you have any question in your mind about whether you are truly hungry, wait to eat.
Let the growl get stronger.
If you have any question about whether you are getting full, stop eating immediately.
Err on the side of pleasing God.
Receive your smiley face sticker!
The worst that can happen is you get to eat again when your stomach growls again soon!
It's no big deal!!!
You are not going to die.
In fact, you'll probably feel really, really great!

DAY TWENTY-NINE: Food Lust

You can't use the words "food" and "lust" together, can you? Lust is just about sexual matters, right? WRONG.

What we see with our eyes and crave with our hearts is lust. Today, we ask God to remove any and all cravings and lusts of our eyes. Notice the use of the words "anything" and "everything" in today's scripture.

Do not love the world or anything in the world. If anyone loves the world, the love of the Father is not in him. For everything in the world—the cravings of sinful man, the lust of his eyes, and the boasting of what he has and does— comes not from the Father but from the world. The world and its desires will pass away, but the man who does the will of God lives forever.
-1 John 2:15-17

This is shocking. We shouldn't love anything the world has to offer. Now, it doesn't say we can't enjoy what the world has to offer. We just shouldn't LOVE things of the world. In my case, food and clothes primarily. The cravings are dangerous. When I start having cravings, it's a sure sign that I'm slipping. Our love should be reserved for the One who IS LOVE. *(1 John 4:8)*

Praise God that He gives us advanced warnings about temptations. He gave me a dream where

I repented of something, and after making me say exactly what I did, He simply smiled and hugged me. It was an image of His forgiveness and gentleness. We can cling to that in moments of soul sorrow.

We can get back on the wagon, bound for the land of milk and honey! A completely fresh start. No looking back. No replaying the mistake in the DVD player of our minds!

There is now no condemnation for those who are in Christ Jesus... -Romans 8:1

<u>Practical Tip of the Day:</u>
Lust is born in the eyes. So don't look if you don't have to!
Steer clear of buffets when possible.
It's almost impossible not to overeat at a buffet for many reasons:
One, there is so MUCH!
Two, you want to get your money's worth.
Three, everyone else is pigging out.
Don't go grocery shopping when you are hungry either. You will look at everything with different eyes and different emotions.
Go when you're full, and you will shop without emotion.
You will make rational decisions based on your budget rather than rash decisions based on greed.
Your heart will not be as prone to lusting after the food.

DAY THIRTY: Fasting

OK, you are ready for this! I'm going to give you proof that God wants us to fast.

1. Jesus did it.
   After fasting forty days and nights, He was hungry. -Matthew 4:2

2. Jesus told us to do it. Notice in this next verse that He says, "WHEN you fast..." not "IF you fast..."
   "When you fast, do not look somber as the hypocrites do, for they disfigure their faces to show men they are fasting. I tell you the truth, they have received their reward in full." -Matthew 6:16

3. The Father rewards it.
   When you fast, put oil on your head and wash your face, so that it will not be obvious to men that you are fasting, but only to your heavenly Father, who is unseen, and your Father, who sees what is done in secret, will reward you. -Matthew 6:17-18

4. It prepares us spiritually for a new work of God in our lives.
   While they were worshiping the Lord and fasting, the Holy Spirit said, "Set apart for me Barnabas and Saul for the work to

which I have called them." So after they had fasted and prayed, they placed their hands on them and sent them off. -Acts 13:2-3

5. Fasting gives us spiritual and mental clarity for times when we desperately need to hear from God about our circumstances or decisions.
   Paul and Barnabas appointed elders for them in each church, and with prayer and fasting, committed them to the Lord, in whom they had put their trust. -Acts14:23

6. Fasting puts us in the right humble state before God.
   They repay me evil for good and leave my soul forlorn. Yet when they were ill, I put on sackcloth and humbled myself with fasting. -Psalm 37:12-13

There is spiritual power in fasting that I cannot explain, but I know it's true. When someone offers a sacrifice of any kind to God in faith, it pleases Him. We draw close to Him by fasting with the right motive, and He blesses with His presence and direction.

We should always let God lead the fast, determining when, why, how long, and what kind of fast it should be. It should never be a ritual or another to-do on our spiritual checklist.

Practical Tip of the Day:
A fast is usually associated with food, but it can be abstaining from anything that would be a true sacrifice. One could fast from caffeine or television.

What does a total fast mean? That's abstaining from all foods and drinking only water. There are all kinds of other fasts, like juice-only fasts and "Daniel" fasts where someone eats only fruits and veggies.
A fast can be any length, even one meal. God accepts any offering made from the heart. Remember this is NOT starving oneself. It's an offering of love for the purpose of prayer.

DAY THIRTY-ONE: Sweet Contentment

I want things to happen immediately. God is teaching me a lot about waiting on Him. Not only that, but being content in the waiting. It's so hard!

One of the ways He's teaching me this is by making me wait until my stomach growls to eat. I can jump ahead of God when I start predicting that my stomach is "about to growl." I confess that I can get downright grumpy at times when I want to eat. That's not of God. A sign of freedom is not being aware of how long it's been since I last ate or wondering when I will get to again. Even in prison, the apostle Paul had a grip on contentment in regards to food.

> *I know what it is to be in need, and I know what it is to have plenty. I have learned the secret of being content in any and every situation, whether well fed or hungry, whether living in plenty or in want. I can do everything through Him who gives me strength. - Philippians 4:12-13*

Today, we petition God to show us that kind of contentment–the secret He revealed to Paul's heart. Whether well fed or hungry, let our countenance be radiant with the joy of the LORD. Let our words and manner be sweet and gentle. Let our focus be on helping others not complaining about our own problems.

Fasting is a true test of contentment versus idolatry. When God quickens your spirit to fast, you will know if your heart still belongs to food. You might get angry at the suggestion of giving it up for a time. You may feel miserable. If your heart no longer belongs to food, you will feel detached and able to set it aside without resentment. You will enjoy a sweet time of fellowship with the Lord as you sense His delight over your obedience.

The LORD your God is with you, He is mighty to save. He will take delight in you, He will quiet you with His love, He will rejoice over you with singing. -Zephaniah 3:17

Just bask in that for a moment, will you please? God Almighty rejoices over you with singing! He sings over you!!! He sings because of you!! That is too wonderful for words. Take a moment and pray for God to press that into the soil of your heart.

<u>Practical Tip of the Day:</u>
Don't watch the clock to decide when to eat.
So many of us, even my own daughter,
will say, "It's 12:15 p.m. We're 15
minutes late for lunch!"
Yet, she's not even hungry. She's just
bought into the cultural lie that you
have to eat at 12 p.m.
It shows me how conditioned we are to
eating according to the clock.
If your family members demand dinner at
a certain time, make sure you are hungry.
Adjust your earlier meal accordingly by the

Spirit to make sure your fuel tank hits "E"
by the dinner bell.
Don't eat just because Big Ben is chiming.

DAY THIRTY-TWO: Free Indeed

If the Son sets you free, you are free indeed.
-John 8:36

This is where I make my big confession: I haven't been walking in total freedom from food like I once did. That doesn't make anything I've told you untrue. It's all God's truth. It simply means that somewhere along the journey, I gave some ground back to the enemy.

The lie that got me in trouble was this: Once you are free, you can never be bound again.

Logically, we understand that a former alcoholic will always have to avoid beer. There is always the possibility that he will fall back into that old temptation.

So it is with an addiction to food. There can be a total freedom in Christ. Yes, indeed. That's God's Truth in John 8:36. However, the enemy knows where our weaknesses are, and he will come back eventually with that same temptation. That's why we can never let our guards down and think "I've got this down pat now." I did, and that was the sin of pride. Just let me tell you from experience, finding the freedom once you've had it and lost it, is much harder than finding it the first time.

Here's the thing though: I've never stopped fighting the good fight of faith, and I've never gone back to where I started. I told you I gave ground to the enemy, but he hasn't conquered me. I've never given up and said, "Oh forget it. I'm just going to pig out."

I've never stopped praying for God's help. Instead of walking in total freedom, I have just walked a path of murky half-obedience (which is disobedience), not eating as much *as I want* but more than God says is enough. You don't want to go there.

Honestly, I didn't want to obey God's call to write this book because I've felt like a hypocrite. "How dare I think I'm qualified to give anyone advice in this area??" That's the taunt of Satan to me.

I've been trying to wait until I get a complete sense of freedom again in this area, but you know what? God has allowed this struggle to re-emerge in me partly for your sake.

He wanted me to EXPERIENCE, not just remember, what you feel like. He wanted me to walk this journey with you day-by-day, and I am. We are in the same boat.

God doesn't need my help to help you. He could deliver you directly, but for some reason He chooses to use imperfect people to accomplish His purposes on the earth. I am certainly one of those imperfect people.

I think about Moses' escape from Egypt in Exodus 2. He was free and clear of Pharoah.

He had started a new life in Midian with a wife and family. Happy Days. But...

The Israelites groaned in their slavery and cried out, and their cry for help because of their slavery went up to God. -Exodus 2:23

It was not Happy Days for the Israelites. God was sending Moses back to that place of slavery.

So now, go. I am sending you to Pharaoh to bring my people the Israelites out of Egypt. But Moses said to God, "Who am I that I should to go Pharaoh and bring the Israelites out of Egypt?" -Exodus 3:10-11

I am not qualified to write this book. That's true, but it's not my book. It's God's.

And He is perfectly able to use anyone, even me, to share His heart of Truth and freedom.

This is what you are to say to the Israelites: "I AM has sent me to you." -Exodus 3:14

I have come to believe that my freedom is tied to yours. God is blessing me with a greater sense of freedom in the obedience of writing this than I've had in a long time. God's mercy is fresh as a daisy in my life today. The Son has set me free, and I am free indeed!

DAY THIRTY-THREE: Thorn in My Side

God is love.

He is actively loving you and me today and every day. Think of what that means. He is ACTIVELY loving you. He is constantly working for your benefit. Sometimes it may not seem that way when things "go wrong" in life. We tell people, "I know God has a plan," but in our hearts we're thinking, "God, you dropped the ball!"

He didn't. He hasn't. He never will. Again I say, God is constantly at work in your life, orchestrating every little detail to do good for you. I've told you before that Romans 8:28 tells us that God works all things for the good of those who love Him and are called according to His purpose. So, when we are struggling with a food temptation, we can be sure it's for our own good. What? Yes, He is allowing us to struggle against overeating. Why? For our own good.

In ways we can't see, He is making us perfect like His Son.

This is one of those somewhat painful truths, like a thorn in our side. Though we beg and plead with God to take away our weakness, He leaves it with us. That doesn't seem very loving or good. Oh, but it is! Read this story carefully:

> *To keep me from becoming conceited because of these surpassingly great revelations, there was given me a thorn in my flesh, a messenger*

of Satan, to torment me. Three times I pleaded with the Lord to take it away from me. But He said to me, "My grace is sufficient for you, for my power is made perfect in weakness." Therefore I will boast all the more gladly about my weaknesses, so that Christ's power may rest on me. That is why, for Christ's sake, I delight in weaknesses..... For when I am weak, then I am strong. -2 Corinthians 12:7-10

Did you get it? It's in our weaknesses that God shows His POWER! If I had been a great piano player since age six, no one now would be saying, "Wow... God really does miracles!!" But if I struggled through piano lessons for years and years with little fruit, then began praying for God's help; and suddenly I began to play with ease, people would have evidence that God is alive, well, and WORKING in my life.

It's the same with food. If this is our natural weakness, but God intervenes, people will notice the miracle. WE will notice the miracle most of all. It builds our faith more than anything to overcome that temptation! Then we have the great joy of telling others that His grace is sufficient. Though I still struggle, His grace is sufficient for me.

I don't give up, and the struggle itself keeps me constantly aware of my need for a Savior, for Jesus. It's for my own good.

Practical Tip of the Day:
Look at your plate differently.
Even if you don't really believe it at
first, try saying, "Wow. I can't possibly
eat all of this."
It will become God's truth for you.
You will find yourself packing up leftovers.
Remember, God is constantly and
actively loving you.
He is working for us, but we have to
cooperate.
I don't know what happens spiritually when
we sleep, but something re-sets itself.

EACH morning, we must choose to be free
and to follow Jesus, wearing that full armor.
We absolutely CANNOT depend on (our
own) yesterday's promises to carry us today!

DAY THIRTY-FOUR: Holy Heads-Up!

I hope you've seen the movie <u>Finding Nemo</u>. It was so full of spiritual concepts. At one point, the two main fish, Marlin and Dory, have to decide whether to go through the scary trench or over it. Dory had been warned not to swim over it, even though it looked really scary to go in.

She had a little short-term memory loss problem, so Marlin didn't trust her judgment.

"Little red flag going up here," Dory said looking at the trench. Something inside her knew which way led to danger. (Dory was clearly a believer.) Doubting Marlin leaned on his own fish wisdom and ended up "taking on the jellies."

Trust in the LORD with all your heart and lean not on your own understanding; in all your ways acknowledge Him, and He will make your path straight. Do not be wise in your own eyes; fear the LORD and shun evil. This will bring health to your body and nourishment to your bones.
-Proverbs 3:5-8

One of the functions of the Holy Spirit is to give us a holy heads-up when we're on a path to trouble. Like Dory's "little red flag," the Holy Spirit will give you a sinking feeling as a warning sign. It very well may go against human wisdom or logic. God is not the least bit impressed by either of those!

For my thoughts are not your thoughts, neither are your ways my ways," declares the LORD. "As the heavens are higher than the earth, so are my ways higher than your ways and my thoughts than your thoughts."
-Isaiah 55:8-9

God likes to work in ways that are counter to our way of thinking. When we choose to rely on God's leading rather than human logic, it again builds our faith. The reality of His love becomes ever more apparent and intimate! We can shout, "Wow! You really care about ME!!!"

"I am the LORD your God, who teaches you what is best for you, who directs you in the way you should go." - Isaiah 48:17

And it's clear that it's completely foolish to ignore that love tap on our conscience.

There is a way that seems right to a man but in the end it leads to death. -Proverbs 14:12

It's an exceedingly joyful thing to know the Holy Spirit shows you that you're about to be tempted, and you can steer clear of trouble. You say, "Oh no, I'm not going there! That's not where God is!" Remember, He can see the Devil's schemes coming a thousand miles away.

Practical Tip of the Day:

Keep your armor on during party time!
It is SO, SO, SO easy for us to drop our
guard at a party. (I did it today at a baby
shower.)

We're chatting, laughing, and mindlessly
popping the yummy and abundant snacks
into our mouths. At the end of the evening,
we can't even remember all that we've
eaten! God can. He's not a kill-joy, but He
wants to help us choose His ways. Make a
plate. Chat *away* from the food table. Don't
get drunk. It only makes it harder to follow
God. (Ephesians 5:17-18)

DAY THIRTY-FIVE: Wide Open Doors of Opportunity

Have you gotten the question yet? "***When are you going to be done*????**"

You might want to ask in response, "Done what? Being obedient to God???" But don't go there. If you haven't been asked the question (or one like it) yet, you will. Prepare your answer now.

You might feel like they're picking a fight or trying to insult you, but your battle is not against flesh and blood. That question is actually a big, wide-open door to share the testimony of what God is doing in your heart and your body.

> *Always be prepared to give an answer to everyone who asks you to give the reason for the hope that you have. But do this with gentleness and respect, keeping a clean conscience, so that those who speak maliciously against your good behavior in Christ may be ashamed of their slander. It is better, if it is God's will, to suffer for doing good than for doing evil.*
> *-1 Peter 3:15-17*

When you are obedient to share your testimony, miracles happen. It's as simple as that.

You want to overcome the enemy? Tell someone what God has done for you.

*They overcame him by the blood of the Lamb
and by the word of their testimony....
-Revelation 12:11*

Sharing our testimony can release a miracle in the life of our hearer; but it surely releases miracles into our lives. I remember one day after I shared my testimony, I went to Walmart. I know God took at least five pounds away from me that day because when I came out of the Walmart restroom, I literally thought I had forgotten to button my jean shorts because they were so loose!

That's what happens when you are faithful to use your weight loss to tell the Truth about WHO is helping you. It's just one of the many millions of ways God can and will work in someone's life so they might have a practical, useful, personal, and specific hope to share in common with an unbeliever.

I'll grant you, it's a little weird when someone asks, "How are you losing weight?" to answer, "Well, Jesus is feeding me." So please don't do that! Be real. Tell them it feels weird to say so, but the truth is that you are praying for God's help to only eat when your body is truly hungry and to stop when it is satisfied. You have nothing to be ashamed of.

*Do your best to present yourself to God as
one approved, a workman who does not need
to be ashamed and who correctly handles the
word of truth. -2 Timothy 2:15*

If anyone is ashamed of me and my words, the Son of Man will be ashamed of him when he comes in His glory... -Luke 9:26

<u>Practical Tip of the Day</u>:
Leveling out is a place for seeking God even more.
You will come to plateaus, places where the scale seems to get stuck.
This isn't the time for *you* to decide whether *you* are satisfied with your weight.
It's not about you. It's time to press in deeper and seek God about whether you have been truly obedient, or if there is still room for improvement. He will let you know. Don't quit.

DAY THIRTY-SIX: What's it Worth?

Have you ever been so hungry that you think you would have given anything for some food? We've just got to know and accept that hunger is a powerful force, and it is from God.

He gave it to us to protect us from starvation. But you know we get carried away. We are often willing to give up too much for the sake of feeding ourselves.

There was a fella in the Bible who made that mistake. His name was Esau. He was the firstborn son of Abraham's promised son Isaac. Isaac loved Esau because he had a taste for wild game, and Esau was a skilled hunter. (Now you can already see that food cravings play a big part in the family dynamic.) Esau's twin (yet younger) brother, Jacob, apparently was a cook with an ambitious eye and the stew to make things happen.

> *Once when Jacob was cooking some stew, Esau came in from the open country, famished. He said to Jacob, "Quick, let me have some of that red stew! I'm famished! Jacob replied, "First sell me your birthright."*
>
> *"Look, I am about to die," Esau said. "What good is the birthright to me?"*
>
> *But Jacob said, "Swear to me first." So he swore an oath to him, selling his birthright to Jacob. Then Jacob gave Esau some bread and some lentil stew. He ate and drank, and*

then got up and left. So Esau despised his birthright. -Genesis 25:29-34

Now before we judge young Esau too harshly for throwing his rightful inheritance away on some lentil stew, we have to do some self-examination. Have there been times when we wanted something to eat so badly that we would have given anything to get it? Don't answer too quickly. I mean times when your tummy has been crawling with hunger pangs, and someone had your very favorite food "Hot Now" as Krispy Kreme says. Truthfully, I don't want to think what stupidity I'm capable of if put under the right pressure.

But it's not worth it. It never is. Did you see how Esau felt after he ate? Stupid and angry. Before we get the food, it seems like the biggest, most impor-tant, and sure-to-be most wonderful thing ever. After we eat, it was just stew. And we can't figure out why we cared so much about it. I believe God gave us this account of Jacob and Esau to witness to us that in the face of our greatest food temptation, IT JUST ISN'T WORTH IT. The hunger pangs are deceiving. They make promises that the food can't keep. Five minutes after we're done eating, the momentary pleasure is over. And, the sin hangover begins.

<u>Practical Tip of the Day:</u>
Find a prayer/accountability partner to walk this journey with you.
So many people are struggling with weight issues, it shouldn't be hard to find someone.

Invite them to do this daily devotion with you. Believe me, even when you get to Day 40, you're not "done." You're never "done." It's not about being DONE!
If by some miracle you don't know anyone who is currently struggling with weight issues, pray for God to send you a same-sex prayer partner. It's never a good idea to have a prayer partner of the opposite sex if you are married (except if it's your own husband). Prayer is the most intimate act you can perform with another person. It ties souls together. Choose wisely who you allow to become that much a part of your soul.

DAY THIRTY-SEVEN: Less is More

I have been physically full to the gills and completely spiritually empty at the same time.

God's fullness is not the same as stomach fullness, but we can be tricked into thinking it is. They are non-transferrable, but we sometimes act like filling our faces might bring us God's peace and joy. It ain't gonna happen. God is too good to let us settle for such a lame substitute for His love.

I want you to know that even if you haven't experienced God's fullness yet, it is still a reality for you. It is promised, and God never, ever goes back on His Word.

For in Christ all the fullness of the Deity lives in bodily form, and you have been given fullness in Christ, who is the head over every power and authority. -Colossians 2:9-10

I went on vacation with four other families one summer. These people are my spiritual family. We truly live life together. Our children are growing up together. The vacation week at the cabin in the North Georgia mountains was awesome. We studied God's Word together each morning, played all day and entered into spontaneous times of worship. It was a little glimpse of heaven.

About mid-week, we had a day of bringing our sins before God and asking forgiveness and cleansing. We all spent extra time alone with the Lord that day, seeking His face. Some were fasting. That afternoon, we got an answer to a prayer we had all been praying together for months. It literally came in the form of a phone call! The fullness of God came upon me like I'd never experienced before except on the day I was saved. I was so spiritually full, I literally could not eat. I tried. Believe me, there was plenty of wonderful food prepared for dinner that I wanted to enjoy. I just couldn't. I was completely and utterly overwhelmed by God's love.

Now, that was an especially powerful time, but God's fullness is available and promised to us each and every day. It is within us. Most of the time, we simply don't have the faith to take God at His Word. So right now, I ask God to increase our faith and pray this verse over us.

And I pray that you, being rooted and established in love, may have power, together with all the saints, to grasp how wide and long and high and deep is the love of Christ, and to know this love that surpasses knowledge — that you may be filled to the measure of all the fullness of God.
-Ephesians 3:17-19

Practical Tip of the Day:
What is physical fullness?
It's less than we think. Less is more.
It's not the result of greed.
It's the result of gratitude.
It's comfortable.
It is not stuffed.

It means I can bend down and tie my shoes
after I eat without holding my breath or
hurting myself!
It's not looking ahead to the next time I can
eat.
That's a healthy look at full.

DAY THIRTY-EIGHT: A Jealous God

Picture this: You're a parent. You helped bring a child into the world. She has your DNA. She looks like you. She makes you laugh. You love everything about her. You love just watching her sleep. She has your heart.

One day, a guy comes along who has nothing but evil intentions towards your child. She begins avoiding you to spend time with him. For some unknown reason, she is drawn to this creep, but you know the truth. He's going to hurt her; maybe even kill her.

How do you feel? What does it do to your stomach? What does it do to your blood?

I described this scenario to explain this spiritual truth: Our God is a jealous God.

...for I, the LORD your God, am a jealous God. -Exodus 20:5

What you would feel in that situation is godly jealousy. It is the heart of a parent to protect a child from harm. So also it is the heart of God to protect His children.

Believe it or not, God Almighty has that kind of fiery passion to protect you from harm. Satan is the creep who wants to draw you away from your heavenly Father, who calls you the apple of His eye. He simply cannot stand by and watch us worship another god, and that's what food can be.

Do not worship any other god, for the LORD, whose name is Jealous, is a jealous God. - Exodus 34:14

For the LORD your God is a consuming fire, a jealous God. -Deuteronomy 4:24

Don't miss the intensity of His emotions when we give our love to something or someone above Him. Process the words "consuming fire." Understand that His **name** is Jealous. That gives us an idea how much a part of His nature it is.

Don't confuse God's kind of jealousy with our own lame, immature, insecure, human jealousy. God is completely secure in who He is. It just breaks His heart to see you walk away from the best, searching for something better. Paul could relate.

I am jealous for you with a godly jealousy. I promised you to one husband, to Christ, so that I might present you as a pure virgin to Him. But I am afraid that just as Eve was deceived by the serpent's cunning, your minds may somehow be led astray from your sincere and pure devotion to Christ. -2 Corinthians 11:2-3

We can see here that God looks at idolatry like adultery. Forgive us, Lord Jesus. Let us not be led astray for even a day. Hide your Word in our hearts that we might not sin against you!

Practical Tip of the Day:

Use a small bowl or plate. A small portion on a big plate looks like a diet. You are not on a diet. A full (small) bowl looks like an abundance. It's easier not to overeat if you don't have to throw food away at the end of the meal. If you're like me, the wasting of food almost kills you!

DAY THIRTY-NINE: Heart Rate

It's time to allow God to rate your heart when it comes to this whole process. The book is almost over, but our journey has really just begun. We have the rest of our lives to choose daily to walk in the freedom of Christ. It's a good time to take our spiritual pulse and examine what is making us tick.

So, let's get personal. Why are you reading this?

Is it because someone else told you to?

Is it a brain exercise that makes you feel better because at least your *reading* about how to lose weight?

Is it because you're so disgusted with your appearance that you'll give any weight loss plan a try?

Or is it God's very Word of life extended to you in a simple way that helps you fight and overcome your temptation to overeat?

Oh, how I pray that's your final answer! Did you notice that I didn't ask you if you've lost weight? I don't even want to know. I would be too easily tempted to take credit for it somehow because of my own sin nature. You might even want to thank me for writing something that helped you. Please don't do that. There are close to 100 scriptures in this book. That's what did the work in you. God Himself reached down and helped you. Pour out your heartfelt thanks to Him every day.

Speaking of self-glorification, how is your heart when it comes to appearing thinner? It's something we have to let God examine carefully because pride sneaks in so fast! Keep in mind God is never looking at your body in a mirror to see how well your jeans fit.

The LORD does not look at the things man looks at. Man looks at the outward appearance, but the LORD looks at the heart. -1 Samuel 16:7

I told you in Day 16, and I remind you now: <u>Man</u> is looking closely at your outward appearance. There will be some who don't like what they see. They will feel convicted by your obedience. They will want to call it something else to take the pressure off themselves.

If you have lost weight rapidly under the hand of God, the only human explanation they will be able to come up with is that you're starving yourself or taking diet pills. You know that's not true. God knows that's not true. They may not believe you, which can be very frustrating, but it's OK. Say what God prompts you to say as a testimony of His power, and leave it at that.

You must speak my words to them, whether they listen or fail to listen, for they are rebellious.
-Ezekiel 2:7

I tell you now, in this life you will have trouble. Whether it's worrying about people saying you're fat, or worrying about people saying you're too skinny.... It's two sides of the same vain coin. You will have trouble in this world. Being thin isn't the answer to life's problems.

> *I have told you these things so that in me you may have peace. In this world you will have trouble. But take heart! I have overcome the world." -John 16:33*

<u>Practical Tip of the Day:</u>
Who cares what people think!

DAY FORTY: The Day of Promise

The 40-day period is a big deal in the Bible.

Noah's flood lasted 40 days. (Genesis 7:4)

Moses spent 40 days on the mountain with God. (Exodus 24:18)

The prophet Elijah traveled 40 days after being strengthened by an angel to escape death.

(1 Kings 19:8)

God gave Ninevah 40 days to repent through the Prophet Jonah (who smelled fishy from his own rebellion). (Jonah 3:4)

Jesus was tempted 40 days by the Devil. (Matthew 4:2)

I knew this book was supposed to be 40 days of devotions for that reason. I had no clue what I could possibly write to fill 40 days, but God was clear that it had to be 40 not 30 or 31, which would have been enough for one month. Men say a habit can be formed in 30 days; God says He works in 40's. I truly encourage you to go read all those wonderful stories, not just the individual verses I mentioned. Ask God to show you why 40 was the time period He required in those situations.

So if you're here, be confident God has done a work in you, no matter what the scale says.

If the scale has revealed lower and lower numbers, I don't say "Congratulations!" I say, "Beware." I don't mean to rain on your parade. I do rejoice with you over a renewed health in your body. I really do!

But the scriptures are very clear about the pitfalls of pride and how we humans tend to behave once we've reached the Promised Land.

It is a land where food is plentiful and nothing is lacking......

When you have eaten your fill, praise the Lord your God for the good land He has given you. But that is the time to be careful! Beware that in your plenty you do not forget the Lord your God and disobey His commands, regulations, and laws. For when you become full and prosperous and have built fine homes to live in, and when your flocks and herds have become very large...

That is the time to be careful. Do not become proud at that time and forget the Lord your God.

-Deuteronomy 8:9-14

If you haven't experienced consistent victory in Christ yet, I tell you, "Congratulations!" Don't give up! Sometimes God works in a gradual process. It might be during your second or third read-thru that God turns on the light bulb in your heart to illuminate these life-changing truths about eating differently.

In the meanwhile, know that God has done a work in you too. Your heart has changed. You have thought about Him more than you ever have before. You have heard your Bridegroom knock. You have heard His voice. You have opened the door and invited Him in to eat with you. You stand today **humble** before the majesty of the King of Kings. He is enthralled with your beauty, and he's not looking at what the world sees. His view is eternally deeper. He delights in His Bride.

Discouragement is not an option, dear one. He has waged war on hell itself to win you as His prize... His most treasured possession. Remain humble and He will lift you up in due time.

It's time to begin again. In fact, as soon as I finish writing Day 40, I'm going to start reading Day One again myself! It's very interesting to me that by the time this book is published, I will have celebrated my 40th birthday. It's not odd; it's GOD.

It's been wonderful visiting with you, but you'll have to excuse me now.

I hear Someone knocking at my door....

CPSIA information can be obtained
at www.ICGtesting.com
Printed in the USA
BVHW080233241221
624759BV00008B/605

9 781607 915089